simply
numerology

simply

numerology

ANNE CHRISTIE

A Sterling / Zambezi Book

Sterling Publishing Co., Inc.

New York

Library of Congress Cataloging-in-Publication Data Available

2   4   6   8   10   9   7   5   3

Published in 2005 by Sterling Publishing Co., Inc.
387 Park Avenue South, New York, NY 10016
Copyright © 2005 Anne Christie
Illustrations Copyright © 2005 Hannah Firmin
Published and distributed in the UK solely by Zambezi Publishing Limited
P.O. Box 221, Plymouth, Devon PL2 2YJ
Distributed in Canada by Sterling Publishing
C/o Canadian Manda Group, 165 Dufferin Street
Toronto, Ontario, Canada M6K 3H6
Distributed in Australia by Capricorn Link (Australia) Pty. Ltd.
P.O. Box 704, Windsor, NSW 2756, Australia

For information about custom editions, special sales, premium and
corporate purchases, please contact Sterling Special Sales
Department at 800-805-5489 or specialsales@sterlingpub.com.

Sterling ISBN 13: 978-1-4027-2277-6
ISBN 10: 1-4027-2277-X

contents

Numerology is nothing more than an amusing game to most people, but for some it is a subject worthy of serious study. People have studied numerology for many thousands of years in order to understand themselves and to unravel the mysteries of the future in much the same way as they have used astrology. In common with the signs and symbols of astrology, numbers appear to contain a universal language. Many early civilizations, such as the ancient Egyptians, the Hebrews, the Chaldeans, and the Hindus, studied numbers as a science. Many believed that everything hides in numbers and that a person who understands their energies can discover their secret.

Numerology has always had a mystical or spiritual significance, and the two main sources of current systems are the Greek philosopher, mathematician, and astrologer Pythagoras and the Hebrew Kabala.

Sometimes called the father of numerology, Pythagoras spent a large part of his working life concentrating on the study of numbers. He was convinced that numbers had mystical properties, and he defined the system of classification that we still use today. In math, every schoolchild learns to recognize the geometrical theories that Pythagoras formulated. Pythagoras believed that numbers contained the secrets of the entire universe, based on the idea that the most powerful (masculine) numbers were the odd ones, while the even numbers were less powerful (and feminine). This actually links with the I Ching, but it is hard to see how Pythagoras could have learned this from Chinese thinkers.

The philosopher Henry Agrippa devised a system that related man to numbers. Count Cagliostro invented his own system that gave prophetic readings. (If you wish to know how his numerological ideas worked, you will find them in a book called *The Lucky Day Finder* in America and Australia, and *The Star Date Oracle* in the UK and Ireland. This book is by my friends Sasha Fenton and Jonathan Dee.)

Both these men based their systems on the ancient Kabalistic system of numerology. Other students of the occult believed that when one transcribed the letters of a person's name into numbers, the results were similar to an astrological chart. One of the most famous numerologists of the nineteenth century was Count Louis Hamon, whom we know by the pen name of Cheiro. Modern people know Cheiro as the author of two famous books on palmistry, but he was an expert on fortune-telling systems. Many famous and influential clients consulted Cheiro, including King Edward VII.

So now, use this simple book to work out your character and destiny and also those of your friends.

1

HOW TO USE NUMBERS

The easiest number alphabet is the Pythagorean or Western system. The alternate Kabalistic system excludes the number nine. Some Hebrews believed that this number represented God, which meant that they used it only for sacred purposes. Other Hebrew scholars called it the "devil's number." Both these strange ideas came from the peculiar way in which the number nine works, because the digits of any multiple of nine always add up to nine. Try it yourself with any multiple of nine that you can think of—it always works.

GOD'S NUMBER OR THE DEVIL'S NUMBER?

18: 1 + 8 = 9
27: 2 + 7 = 9
36: 3 + 6 = 9
45: 4 + 5 = 9
54: 5 + 4 = 9
63: 6 + 3 = 9

63 x 72 = 4536
4 + 5 + 3 + 6 + = 18
1 + 8 + = 9

YOUR BASIC TOOL KIT

Using numbers together with the table of keywords, you will be able to look at your own character and study the temperament of others. It requires no special talent or psychic skill, and you do not have to be a mathematician to understand it, because there are no formulas or equations to memorize. Numerology is fun, simple, yet scientific, so it will enable you to pinpoint areas that you can work on for your personal growth.

THE NAME NUMBER

Old-time numerologists used to insist that when you look into the vibrations of your name, you use the one that is on your birth certificate. Many modern numerologists consider this a waste of time unless you continue to use your birth name throughout your life. People change their names for many reasons or even use one name in private and a pen name or some other name for their work. You may use a shortened version of your name, such as Jackie or Mike. Why not try the system using your birth name and any other names that you have used along the way? Then you can see whether these name changes have affected your behavior at different times of your life or under different circumstances, such as before or after marriage.

You may wish to copy the table illustrated below for your own use, so that it is easy to refer back to, until you become familiar with it.

1	2	3	4	5	6	7	8	9
A	B	C	D	E	F	G	H	I
J	K	L	M	N	O	P	Q	R
S	T	U	V	W	X	Y	Z	

Work out the number that corresponds to each letter in your name, make a note of it, then shrink the number down to a single digit by adding the numbers together. Just study the following example and you will soon get the idea. I have used an imaginary person called James Robert Pearson for this purpose. The first thing we must do is find the numbers that correspond to every letter in James's name.

James   Robert   Pearson
1, 1, 4, 5, 1   9, 6, 2, 5, 9, 2   7, 5, 1, 9, 1, 6, 5

Now James needs to add all the numbers together to see what they come to. He can do it all at once, or one piece at a time. Here are both methods:

James Robert Pearson
$1 + 1 + 4 + 5 + 1 + 9 + 6 + 2 + 5 + 9 + 2 + 7 + 5 + 1 + 9 + 1 + 6 + 5 = 79$

James Robert Pearson
James: $1 + 1 + 4 + 5 + 1$ $= 12$
Robert: $9 + 6 + 2 + 5 + 9 + 2$ $= 33$
Pearson: $7 + 5 + 1 + 9 + 1 + 6 + 5 = 34$
                                         79

Now we reduce this number by adding 7 and 9 to make 16.

Then we reduce the number again by adding 1 and 6 to make 7.

Thus, James Robert Pearson's name number is seven.

Let us assume that James Robert Pearson prefers to call himself Jim Pearson and see what happens:

Jim Pearson
Jim: 1 + 9 + 4 = 14
Pearson: 7 + 5 + 1 + 9 + 1 + 6 + 5 = 34
48

Now we add 4 and 8 to make 12.

Then add 1 and 2 to make 3.

Thus, Jim Pearson's name number is three.

THE ENERGY OF NUMBERS— KEY WORDS

One	Personal resources
Two	Personal feelings
Three	Personal creativity
Four	Instinct and logic
Five	Expansion and sense
Six	Intuition and theory
Seven	Setting limits
Eight	Transformation
Nine	Spiritual creativity

2+1+2+9+5

THE COLOR CODE

Each number corresponds to a specific color, so once you understand the vibrational energies of the numbers, you can choose to wear certain colors to tap into them.

One	Light green	The physical body
Two	Dark green	The emotions
Three	Pink	Creativity
Four	Black	The material world
Five	Yellow	Intellect
Six	Brown	Effectiveness
Seven	Blue	Communication
Eight	Purple	Spirituality
Nine	White	Higher spirit

NUMBERS AND ASTROLOGY

NUMBER	ENERGY	PLANET	SIGN	KEYWORD
One	Ego	Sun	Leo	Positive
Two	Caring	Moon	Cancer	Feelings
Three	Action	Mars	Aries	Initiative
Four	Instincts	Mercury	Gemini/Virgo	Thought
Five	Learning	Jupiter	Sagittarius	Expansion
Six	Imagination	Venus	Taurus/Libra	Discrimination
Seven	Time	Neptune	Pisces	Intuition
Eight	Transformation	Pluto	Scorpio	Subconscious
Nine	Karma	Neptune	Pisces	Spirituality
Ten	Intellectual	Uranus	Aquarius	Originality

THE DYNAMIC FORCES OF NUMBERS

Masculine and Feminine Numbers

Masculine and feminine numbers (first suggested by Pythagoras) do not have a sexual association. They relate to the dynamic forces that govern the energy of each number.

Masculine	Feminine
One	Two
Three	Four
Five	Six
Seven	Eight
Nine	

THE NUMBER CHAPTERS

Now you can move on and discover what the various numbers can tell you about yourself or about any other person whom you wish to analyze. Certain chapters will show you how you and others are operating right now, but other chapters will show the karma that you brought into the world with you when you were born. This will show the benefits with which you were born and the aspects of your life or yourself on which you might still have to do some work.

Later chapters show you how to predict events; the final chapter offers suggestions about compatibility with other people.

2

NAME NUMBER

Numerological theory suggests that you always use the full name on your birth certificate when working out your name number, but it is also interesting to see how a change of name can affect your outlook. Many women marry and change their name to their husband's family name, but other changes are a matter of choice, or simply a matter of shortening a name; for example, Mike Smith rather than Michael Edward Smith. So try this the first time around by using your birth certificate name, and then try it again with the name you normally go by.

Here is the alphabet table again. Use the examples as shown in the previous chapter and keep reducing your total until you end up with a number between 1 and 9. If you end up with 11 or 22, leave these numbers as they are.

1	2	3	4	5	6	7	8	9
A	B	C	D	E	F	G	H	I
J	K	L	M	N	O	P	Q	R
S	T	U	V	W	X	Y	Z	

NUMBER ONE

Vibration: The Sun

Associated with: Benevolence, creativity, and protection

Sun sign: Leo

Symbol: The lion

Kabala: Unity, wholeness, totality

Keywords: Ego, personal identity, leadership, purposeful, tenacious

Days of the month: 1, 10, 19, 28

Number One people dislike criticism. They have a strong sense of their own worth, so they usually demand and get respect from others. These folk insist on controlling and organizing everyone and everything, and they hold quite definite views, so they can be stubborn when thwarted. There is an underlying desire to be original, creative, and inventive. Anything they undertake can result in a rise to a position of authority, and they often insist that everyone look up to them, and this includes friends and family, colleagues—and even the boss. Without the respect of others, they take out their resentment and frustration on anyone who happens to be around.

A Number One person will shoulder burdens, protect the weak, and defend the helpless, as long as the hapless person does exactly as he is told. These individuals always know better than anyone else does, and they are quite certain that their opinions are flawless. Most of the time, they are right, and this annoys everyone else—especially those who are required to listen to their lectures.

Number One people are very susceptible to sincere compliments. When they know that others genuinely appreciate them, they will do anything to please and they can be outstandingly kind and generous. Love—both giving and receiving—is as vital as breathing to a Number One.

When someone shows them up or wounds their pride, they can become most unpleasant. These individuals will forget slights quite quickly, but only after suitably humble apologies—the only way to end a confrontation with a Number One person. They treat those whom they trust and love with warmth and affection, but familiarity from strangers causes deep resentment.

Number Ones love children and young people. Often there is sadness connected with a child. Clothes, jewels, and flashy cars are a basic requirement. These people have an unmistakable sense of inbred dignity. An ideal career is a creative or manual job that allows a measure of authority and freedom from restriction.

Their weak areas include the heart or circulation, eye trouble, or poor vision.

NUMBER TWO

Vibration:	The Moon
Associated with:	Dreams, conception, childbirth, parenthood, imagination, and sensitivity
Sun sign:	Cancer
Symbol:	The crab
Kabala:	Division, relatedness
Keywords:	Feeling, caring, balanced, sensitive, cheerful, team worker

Days of the month: 2, 11, 20, 29

Number Two people fear the unfamiliar or the unknown. They are not always as forceful as they need to be when carrying out ideas and plans, but they are inventive and imaginative. These people have a romantic nature, and their intuition is often highly developed. They may fear every kind of loss imaginable—love, property, friendship, money, work—or the loss of relationships through separation or death. They love to travel, but they need a secure home base. Often devoted to their parents, particularly their mother, they must be careful not to smother their children by being overly possessive.

All Number Two people are concerned with family and friends. They tend to hover and try to ensure that their loved ones do not make unsuitable friends, catch cold, or throw money away on foolish ventures. They seek partners in love and in business, as they don't always feel that they can cope alone. Ultracautious, they hate gambling or taking chances. Although they love money, they prefer to save it in secure investments and to increase their capital with interest and dividends.

These most secretive individuals never confide in anyone. They manage to wheedle out other people's secrets, but they refuse to let anyone invade their own privacy. They will often appear to be undecided, and then they will make an unexpected move—sometimes with a surprising degree of aggression. Their careers might include teaching, caring for children, or writing stories for children.

Their weak areas are the lungs, breasts, chest, and stomach.

NUMBER THREE

Vibration:	Mars
Associated with:	Service and direct action
Sun sign:	Aries
Symbol:	The ram
Kabala:	Fertility, completion

Keywords: Creative, versatile, adaptable,
                       idealistic, charming

Days of the month: 3, 12, 21, 30

Number Three people want nothing less than the truth—
they cannot be fooled by deception and they can spot a
phony a mile off. Do not attempt to bother them with lies,
dishonesty, or even a mild distortion of the truth. Some
Number Three individuals actually manage to achieve their
ultimate goal of truthfulness, while others mislead themselves into believing their own illusions, and for them the
search for reality never ends.

Fiercely independent, these subjects will not allow others
to tie them down, and they will always demand total
freedom of speech and movement. Travel is a necessity for
them, and they need opportunities to see the world, to learn
about foreign countries, and to mix with a wide variety of
people. Number Three people are passionately interested in
philosophy and intellectual concepts. They have their own
contagious brand of optimism, and they look on the bright
side of everything. These individuals can spend their lives in
a quest for truth, and they can be religious, fiercely
agnostic, or atheist. Because the concept of religion or philosophy is a vital part of their life, it is never a neutral issue
and is either accepted or rejected with fervor or fanaticism.

Expect these individuals to speak bluntly and to offer a direct
and candid opinion. These people show fierce loyalty to their
pets and to all animals and will always defend the underdog
(animal or human) in any dispute. Total freedom within the
ties of marriage and family is the only way for them.

Number Three subjects are attracted to gambling, tests of physical strength, and risk taking in all its forms, and they enjoy playing or watching rough sports. They prefer jobs that allow them to travel; they enjoy being in positions of authority; and they can enjoy working in military or government occupations.

Their personality is a strange blend of the happy-go-lucky clown and the wise philosopher. They can be so two-sided that one day they will be perfectly sensible and the next, almost completely crazy. Their ambitions, dreams, and goals may sometimes be serious and attainable, but often they are just frivolous. Their emotions are in control of their minds, so their attitudes and decisions will depend upon whether they are in the mood to be sensible, jolly, or silly, or whether they have worked themselves into such a rage that they are capable of saying or doing just about anything.

Their weak area is the lower spine, leading to sciatica and skin complaints. They can suffer from nervous problems through overwork.

NUMBER FOUR

Vibration: Mercury

Associated with: Instincts, logic, the material world
                          and the intellect

Sun sign: Gemini/Virgo

Kabala: Solidity, reliability, the law

Symbol: The twins/The virgin

Keywords: Hardworking, sensible, logical, materialistic

Days of the month: 4, 13, 22, 31

Frequently, the family and friends of Number Four people misunderstand them. This is because they make their own enigmatic rules that do not always correspond to those of society. Every thought and action is marked with a peculiar individuality. Their speech and actions shock others, and this often seems to be deliberate. If there is an unconventional way of going about something, the Number Four person will find it. These people care little for the present because their concerns are for the future, so they are frequently light-years ahead of the rest of us. They seem to have an inborn talent for prophecy and for knowing what will happen or what will be fashionable long before it arrives.

The lifestyle of Number Four people is usually unconventional, but their crazy ideas often turn out to be surprisingly successful. The curious nature of these individuals draws them to anything that is off the beaten track. Any incredible, unscientific, or unproven theory excites the Number Four person, and he can convince himself (and everyone else) that a peculiar notion can be turned into reality. Never tell this subject that something is impossible—it simply spurs him on to prove you wrong.

In every area of life, the vibration of Number Four is one of change, but these unusual people are often reluctant to change their own personal habits, as they can be both fixed and stubborn. When others ask them to become more socially acceptable, they resist.

While money has little or no meaning, friendships are vital. The Number Four person has no desire to impress others, and he doesn't even care where he lives, as long as he can keep his imagination intact. These people genuinely fail to notice their surroundings. They believe in "live and let live," but in return, they expect to be given the same consideration by others. They enjoy working in the fields of building, architecture, and design.

Their weak spots are the kidneys and bladder, plus headaches and nervous tension.

NUMBER FIVE

Vibration: Jupiter

Associated with: Expansion, tolerance, communication, versatility, and movement

Sun sign: Sagittarius

Symbol: The archer

Kabala: Life, regeneration, creativity, expansion

Keywords: Education, travel, philosophy,
                     liveliness, creativity, artistry

Days of the month: 5, 14, 23

Number Five people are innately courteous and charming, but if they spot flaws and mistakes, they will not hesitate to point them out. These people cannot ignore their own mistakes or those of others, so they frequently beat themselves up and lay blame on others. Change is a necessity to them in all areas of their lives, and they adore travel and movement. Because it is hard for them to rely on their intuition and feelings, they may overanalyze situations and people. This can cause breakdowns in their relationships, because no partnership can bear the pressure of constant scrutiny. Number Fives can talk a love affair to death. They do not understand that love has nothing to do with logic.

They make pleasant company, because outwardly they are fun and cooperative. Number Five is the vibration of the higher intellect. These are extremely bright people—always mentally alert and having a higher than average intelligence. As they are fine-tuned to notice the tiniest detail, they never miss a trick. They know instinctively how to use the space that they inhabit, and if money pressures prevent them from traveling, they will daydream and travel in their minds. Their vivid imaginations are enough to satisfy their wandering urges.

Traditionally, the Number Five is associated with earth magic. These people often long to believe in magic, fairies, and anything mysterious. However, their need to analyze every detail is at odds with this, so they frequently find it hard to understand themselves.

Number Five people are unusually high-strung. They crave excitement and live on their nerves. Their ability to think and act quickly means that they often act impulsively. At heart, they are speculators with a keen sense for new inventions and a willingness to take risks. Successful occupations are likely to be writing, publishing, advertising, public relations, sales, teaching, speculation, and the travel trade. Those ruled by Number Five are blessed with a flexible point of view. They have the ability to recover from bad experiences and to move on.

Health problems might include insomnia, neuritis, and nervous problems.

NUMBER SIX

Vibration:	Venus
Associated with:	Abstract thinking, fantasy, creativity, and imagination
Sun sign:	Taurus/Libra
Symbol:	The bull/The scales
Kabala:	Fruitfulness, harmony, the home
Keywords:	Imagination, theory, balance, harmony
Days of the month:	6, 15, 24

Number Six people can be magnetically attractive, and their families, friends, and associates genuinely love them. They are devoted to their loved ones, and they know how to show it. Idealism rather than sex motivates the nature of Number Six people, and they are born romantics, with a streak of sentimentality that is impossible for them to deny or hide. They love harmony in their surroundings and they adore music and art. They try to live in beautiful homes with the most tasteful furnishings.

Making others happy and entertaining friends rank high on their personal list of important activities. They cannot face jealousy, discord, arguments, or unpleasantness of any sort. Number Six people make friends easily, and they enjoy settling the disputes of their relatives and friends. They appear to be the most docile and amenable people until they are crossed; then their stubborn nature kicks in.

Money often comes without effort, sometimes through inheritance and sometimes through the way that they use their abilities and talents. They can often veer between extravagance and stinginess. They may work in the arts, the media, entertainment, or some aspect of the health and fitness industry, especially one that is associated with dieting.

Most Number Six people love the countryside and find it emotionally soothing to live or spend time near trees or water. They find anything ugly very offensive, and they are very fond of luxury in all its forms. They hate vulgarity or loud behavior and will always show the highest admiration for anything that is tasteful and refined. These subjects invariably have impeccable manners and are always polite, but they do not hesitate to make their opinions clear whenever they have strong feelings about something. Discussion and debate come easily to them. Their logical minds usually win others over to their point of view. They have an irresistible smile.

Weak spots are the throat, voice, nose, and lungs. They can suffer from circulatory problems, and lack of exercise causes weight gain.

NUMBER SEVEN

Vibration: Neptune

Associated with: The bridge to the spiritual world

Sun sign: Pisces

Symbol: The two fish

Kabala: Mysticism, magic, spirituality

Keywords: Spiritual, sensitive, intuitive

Days of the month: 7, 16, 25

Number Seven people often have amazing dreams. Sometimes they tell others about them and sometimes they just keep quiet about them. They have a secret interest in mysteries, UFOs, and mythology—in fact, they are attracted to anything that is unknown. These people are often intuitive and clairvoyant, with magnetic, calming personalities. These individuals have strange and unorthodox ideas about religion, politics, or just life in general. Following the herd is not for them—although they can be attracted to the latest religious cult.

A Number Seven person will probably become a seasoned traveler who enjoys reading travel books and soaking up information about foreign countries and people. There may be a strong attraction to the sea, so they may take up water sports or sailing or spend their lives at work on the sea.

These individuals prefer to work in the arts or the entertainment industry, and while they can make good money at times, they are aware that their success is likely to be short-lived. They don't bother much with material possessions or money in the normal course of things. They may make significant contributions to charities, but in a quiet way.

It is unlikely to hear Number Seven people talk much about their ambitions, because the things that they involve themselves in have a philosophical tinge. Fortunate friends and family of Number Seven folk know that their loved ones will stand up for them and offer them a sympathetic and understanding ear when they need it.

Here you find a sensitive nature, an artistic temperament, and the most refined manners. These people are truly unprejudiced and nonjudgmental. Never expect to get a Number Seven person to tell you what he or she is really thinking—these individuals live in a world of secret dreams, and they only divulge them to those whom they trust most.

This number is the symbol of the ancient Greek god Chronos, who reminds us that things that have a limited duration are not real. Number Seven is symbolic of totality in the material world—the seven notes in the musical scale, seven colors of the rainbow, seven virtues, seven deadly sins, seven chakras in the body, seven planets known to the ancient world, and seven days of the week.

Skin complaints may be a problem, but bad diet and worry can also make a Number Seven person ill.

NUMBER EIGHT

Vibration: Pluto

Associated with: Practical matters, the unconscious, and transformation

Sun sign: Scorpio

Symbol: The phoenix/scorpion/eagle

Kabala: Material concerns, leadership, justice, ambition

Keywords: Ambitious, self-sufficient, persistent

Days of the month: 8, 17, 26

Number Eight people are reserved and quiet. They are not pushy, but they usually get where they want to go, slowly and surely, so that they achieve their ambitions. Their shy manner is a cover for an intense drive to get to the top. The areas in which the Number Eight operates are money, sex, and power. These individuals are patient people who are quite happy to wait for their plans to bear fruit. It is unusual to find them procrastinating. Their sense of responsibility and duty does not allow them to waste time, and they can be relied on to do what others expect of them. They find careers in public life, any large organization, and jobs that offer challenge and excitement, such as fund-raising and big business.

Their sense of humor is subtle and dry, which makes them amusing company. They may behave as though they don't care what others think of them, but secretly they enjoy compliments and sincere appreciation and they hate to be thought stupid or wrong.

There is an enormous inner strength in most Number Eight people, and they harbor deep, intense natures. They often find that they have an important role to play in the lives of others, and sometimes they can be fanatical about religion. Although they make many loving friends, they also make bitter enemies. They may seem to be undemonstrative and cold toward those whom they love and trust. Although they show affection shyly, in reality they are devoted to their friends and family. Underneath a cool surface lurk loneliness and a desperate need to be loved. When it is necessary, Number Eight people may go to great lengths to make sacrifices for a strongly held ambition or ideal, or for those who depend on them.

With age and maturity, Number Eight people look and behave younger than their years. They demand much of themselves and others, but for all their appearance of discipline, maturity, and self-control, deep down they are needy and lonely. The wholehearted pursuit of happiness is difficult for them.

Their health might include liver problems, rheumatism, headaches, and diseases of the blood.

NUMBER NINE

Vibration:	Neptune
Associated with:	Divine love, completion, talent, spirituality, and karma
Sun sign:	Pisces
Symbol:	The fish
Kabala:	Humanitarian issues, inspirational leadership
Keywords:	Creative, spiritual, compassionate

Days of the month: 9, 18, 27

Number Nine folk are determined to get their own way. They can be impulsive and prone to make snap decisions, and then live to regret their hasty actions. Although Number Nine people have a temper, they soon forgive and forget.

Their trusting nature means that others can lead them into trouble. They are direct and straightforward, they expect others to be the same, and they are disappointed when they discover that others can be manipulative or devious, because they are incapable of such behavior themselves. They need to be more cautious and less trusting. These subjects can be relied upon to show understanding, compassion, and the highest ideals of selfless love. They possess an amazing ability to go straight to the heart of a situation, bypassing the need for lengthy analysis. Slower thinkers get on their nerves. At times, their impatience with others does not win them friends or allies.

These subjects have a touchingly childlike quality of vulnerability that drives others to protect them. Some people may think they are foolish and find it hard to respect them, but once they experience the courageous spirit (and violent temper) of the Number Nine, they think again. Although these people often appear to be vain, their concern about their own appearance derives from lack of confidence and fear of rejection. They may appear to be assertive, independent, and pushy, but in reality they need constant reassurance that others love, like, admire, and respect them.

Often very extravagant and very generous to others, they will instinctively let tomorrow take care of itself—let go of everything and just give. These individuals always tune in to happiness and joy. They choose to work in the spheres of art, writing, music, religious work, theater, and entertainment. Surprisingly, some opt for a career in the military. These folk are excellent advisers.

Health problems relate to fever and Number Nine people have delicate stomachs, possibly owing to nerves and tension.

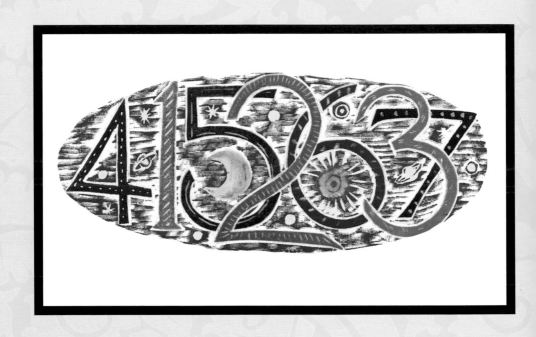

COMPOUND NAME NUMBER

To calculate your compound name number, you can use your popular name or the name on your birth certificate. In this case, we have used our imaginary guinea pig's birth name. This time you need to reduce the name until you have a two-digit number, but the number must be 30 or below.

When we add James Robert Pearson's numbers together, the result comes to 79. This number is above 30, so we continue to reduce it by adding the 7 and 9 to make 16. This is now a two-digit number that is below 30. If this process of reduction bypasses the range between 10 and 30, then this section does not apply to you.

Example: James Robert Pearson
James: 1 + 1 + 4 + 5 + 1   = 12
Robert: 9 + 6 + 2 + 5 + 9 + 2   = 33
Pearson: 7 + 5 + 1 + 9 + 1 + 6 + 5 = 34

James: 12
Robert: 33
Pearson: 34
            79

Now we add 7 and 9 to get 16.

NUMBER TEN
THE WHEEL OF FORTUNE

• Ten is the number of rise and fall; it represents good or evil, depending upon the action the person chooses to take.

- It is the number of extreme responses, such as fear, hate, or respect.

- This number allows a person to understand his power and to use it wisely.

- It represents the power to take a creative concept and turn it into something concrete.

- The subject must be self-disciplined and compassionate.

- This individual must avoid arrogance or lashing out when frustrated.

NUMBER ELEVEN
THE CLENCHED FIST

- This number represents treachery and problems that seem to come from nowhere.

- Number Eleven represents two opposing situations or individuals who may eventually separate, which causes difficulties.

- This person needs to learn to compromise and to avoid those things that cause splits in partnerships and relationships.

- Two separate desires or forces may unite and bring happiness, or they may bring conflict and cause separation.

NUMBER TWELVE
THE VICTIM

- This number represents the victim, who chooses or is forced to make sacrifices so that others can achieve their ends.

- The subject must be alert in every situation and must watch out for false flattery or hidden agendas.

- This person must guard against allowing others to use him for their own gain.

- If this person is offered a position of authority, he must ask why he is being given this opportunity, as it may not be all that it appears to be on the surface.

- In order to achieve intellectual and spiritual wisdom, he will need to make sacrifices and look for solutions from within.

- If he takes the trouble to learn and to gain an education, he will overcome suffering and achieve eventual success, so the number represents education, teachers, and students.

NUMBER THIRTEEN
TRANSFORMATION

- Thirteen is not an unlucky number.

- This person can achieve a position of power and authority.

- This number symbolizes breaking new ground, new discoveries, and explorers.

- The power associated with Number Thirteen can bring personal destruction if it is used selfishly.

- This number warns of the unexpected and unknown.

- This person can use the strength of this vibration to adapt to new circumstances.

NUMBER FOURTEEN CHALLENGE

- This number connects with the media, publishing, and writing.

- Partnerships and businesses will be of great benefit, but the subject must avoid taking what others say on trust, or relying on them.

- Luck comes with speculation; both gains and losses are likely to be temporary.

- This is a fortunate number for travel with others.

- This subject may face danger through the forces of nature, such as fire, floods, tornadoes, and earthquakes.

- This is the number of the inner voice, intuition, and self-reliance.

- The prospect of loss is always present, even though money dealings and speculation can prove lucky, but the individual must guard against overconfidence.

NUMBER FIFTEEN
THE MAGICIAN

- This person can make others happy, and he can shine light into the darkness.

- The individual has a dramatic temperament, personal magnetism, charisma, and eloquence.

- This number is fortunate in obtaining money, favors, and gifts.

- Whenever it is associated with the Numbers Four and Eight, this number can be associated with black magic—or with becoming a victim of magic.

NUMBER SIXTEEN
THE SHATTERED CITADEL

- This number warns of accidents, and it advises the subject to make careful plans before undertaking anything important.

- This person must pay careful attention to detail and anticipate problems.

- Dreams and the person's inner voice may warn him of danger in good time.

- Success and happiness come in strange ways, but not via leadership, fame, or celebrity.

NUMBER SEVENTEEN
THE STAR

- The eight-sided star of Venus is associated with this number, and it represents love and peace.

- Number Seventeen is associated with the ancient magi.

- This number promises a spiritual rise above trials and tribulations as well as the ability to overcome former failures in career and personal relationships.

- This is a fortunate compound number, representing immortality.

NUMBER EIGHTEEN
CONFLICT

- Number Eighteen symbolizes bitter quarrels and family disputes.

- This number warns that going after too many material things can retard one's spiritual growth.

- This is the number of social revolution, wars, and upheaval.

- This number brings warnings of treachery and deception from both enemies and friends.

- Money or status may come as a result of conflict.

- This subject must beware of danger from natural disasters or electric shocks.

- This individual must meet hatred and deception with generosity, forgiveness, love, and kindness, because for him, love will always conquer conflict.

NUMBER NINETEEN
THE SUN

- This is one of the most fortunate of the compound numbers, as it indicates victory over disappointment and failure.

- Any negative vibrations will be diluted by this number, which blesses the individual and promises fulfillment, happiness, and personal success.

- All ventures should go smoothly.

NUMBER TWENTY
JUDGMENT

- Number Twenty symbolizes a powerful awakening, which will bring new purpose, plans, and ambition.

- This number brings a clear a call to action.

- Faith in the personal power to transform will conquer delays.

- This is not the number of financial success, as it applies to personal happiness and achievement.

NUMBER TWENTY-ONE
THE UNIVERSE

- This number brings advancement, awards, and success.

- After a long struggle, there will be victory.

- This number represents the final victory over all opposition, plus karmic rewards.

NUMBER TWENTY-TWO
CAUTION

- This number warns against living in a fool's paradise.

- It represents a dreamer who only wakes up when surrounded by danger.

- There is the clear warning of putting too much faith in others.

- The individual should avoid those who are untrustworthy and should always exercise caution.

- The subject must understand that the power to change things in his life and to prevent failure lies in his own hands, so he must focus on success.

NUMBER TWENTY-THREE THE LION

- This number brings success in career and personal life.

- People in authority offer help and protection.

- This number offers strength, the ability to face challenges, and the ability to win.

NUMBER TWENTY-FOUR CREATIVITY

- This person can expect help from people in authority and positions of power.

- This number brings success, especially in the arts, the law, and love.

- This subject has a magnetic personality, and he can attract lovers.

- Self-indulgence and arrogance can cause disappoint- ments in career, finance, and personal relationships.

- This subject must never allow good fortune make him careless about spiritual values.

- He must resist the temptation to overindulge or to become selfish.

NUMBER TWENTY-FIVE ANALYSIS

- Learning from experience will bring worldly success.

- Disappointments that this subject overcomes in early life will help to make him strong.

- This person has excellent powers of judgment.

NUMBER TWENTY-SIX PARTNERSHIPS

- This number represents helping others, compassion, and an unselfish attitude.

- This subject will suffer disappointment and failure, which are usually brought about by taking bad advice.

NUMBER TWENTY–SEVEN
THE SCEPTER

- This subject will rise to a position of authority.

- This is a fortunate compound number, touched with enchantment, harmony, and courage.

- There are likely to be substantial rewards when the person uses imagination and intellect.

- This person should never allow himself to be intimidated or influenced by the opinions of others.

- It is important for him to bring bright ideas and plans to a conclusion.

NUMBER TWENTY–EIGHT
THE LAMB

- This person can achieve success, but he must guard against later losses, especially from lawsuits.

- Loss comes about through misplaced trust in others and opposition from enemies or competitors in business.

- This individual may have to pull himself up by the boot-straps and start again.

- The phrase "look before you leap" is the key to this number.

NUMBER TWENTY—NINE
GRACE UNDER PRESSURE

- This person must accept responsibility and not blame others when things go wrong.

- A series of trials and tribulations will test this individual's spiritual strength.

- This subject must avoid unreliable friends who can deceive him or make him feel uncertain about his own judgment.

- The opposite sex may be the cause of anxiety and grief.

- This individual must develop an optimistic outlook and learn to believe in himself.

NUMBER THIRTY
MEDITATION

- Success depends upon the person himself, as he has few real friends.

- This subject will learn by going on an inward journey and by considering spiritual rather than material matters.

- This individual may be a loner by nature, or this may be a temporary situation.

- This person can turn his ideas into something worthwhile, and while he may be alone much of the time, it appears that he prefers it that way.

PERSONALITY NUMBER

The personality number represents the face you show to the world. It is best to use the name you usually call your-self when calculating this number.

Count the consonants in your name and ignore the vowels. Reduce the result to a single digit, 11, or 22 for this chapter.

In the case of our imaginary person, Jim Pearson, he would only add together the numbers that represent the letters J, M, P, R, S, and N as follows:

1	2	3	4	5	6	7	8	9
A	B	C	D	E	F	G	H	I
J	K	L	M	N	O	P	Q	R
S	T	U	V	W	X	Y	Z	

J = 1, M = 4, P = 7, R = 9, S = 1, N = 5

1 + 4 + 7 + 9 + 1 + 5 = 27

2 + 7 = 9

Therefore, Jim Pearson's personality number is nine.

NUMBER ONE

- An appearance of confidence usually masks feelings of uncertainty.

- This person is a natural leader who assumes responsibility.

- He has many good friends.

- He may be arrogant and pushy.

- Overdemanding behavior can alienate friends and colleagues.

NUMBER TWO

- This person strives for perfection.

- The search for harmony and balance can attract criticism.

- This individual is hard for others to live with.

- This subject must learn to trust and allow others to be wrong sometimes.

NUMBER THREE

- Loneliness lies behind a cheerful, sociable, popular, confident appearance.

- This individual sometimes dresses very extravagantly.

- This natural actor adores the center stage and has masses of energy.

- He can be boastful and conceited, but this subject is a real softie underneath.

NUMBER FOUR

- A Number Four person is a trustworthy, loyal, dependable partner.

- This individual hates innovation, change, and anything unconventional.

- This subject should chill out, be less conservative.

- This person must allow others to have their opinions.

NUMBER FIVE

- This individual is well read, inquisitive, or a restless gossip.

- He is a great companion and an excellent friend.

- This person may travel a great deal for fun or business purposes.

- Many changes of address and connections with other countries are in store for this individual.

NUMBER SIX

- This individual has an easygoing attitude to life.

- He hates disagreements and problems.

- This person places great value on beauty and luxury.

- This individual is charming, but can sometimes be selfish.

NUMBER SEVEN

- The Number Seven person is reserved and difficult to get to know, standoffish.

- Underneath a cool exterior, this individual reveals an interesting, friendly personality.

- He is often a mine of information on anything related to mysticism.

- This individual may be psychic.

NUMBER EIGHT

- The Number Eight person is demanding and bossy, but hard on himself as well as on others.

- He is a good employer with a shrewd understanding of finances.

- This excellent organizer will always rise to a challenge.

- He loves the best of everything for himself and his family.

NUMBER NINE

- Fun and energetic, this subject exudes charm, sex appeal, and magnetism.

- This person hates restriction, so he has many relationships.

- This individual is a terrible time keeper.

- He is interested in spiritual matters.

NUMBER ELEVEN

- This person makes enemies unintentionally.

- He cannot stand those who disagree with him.

- Given time, this person becomes a faithful, loyal friend.

- This individual needs a secure emotional life.

NUMBER TWENTY—TWO

- The Number Twenty-two person is always ready with help and advice.

- He maintains inner strength and wisdom and has sound judgment.

- This is a happy, attractive person who makes a wonderful friend.

- This subject can be a wonderful builder, designer, or architect

5

HEART NUMBER

The heart number reveals your personal feelings and deepest wishes. Most of us keep these hidden—sometimes even from ourselves—so this number will help you to understand what motivates instinctive behavior and to reveal hidden talents. This makes it easier to understand your true needs when making important decisions. Naturally, it also gives you an idea of where other people are coming from.

It is best to use the name that you usually call yourself for this calculation. If a heart number comes to 11 or 22, leave this rather than reducing the number any further.

To calculate the heart number, use only the vowel numbers of a name. Therefore, in the case of our friend Jim Pearson, he would only add up I, E, A, and O.

1	2	3	4	5	6	7	8	9
A	B	C	D	E	F	G	H	I
J	K	L	M	N	O	P	Q	R
S	T	U	V	W	X	Y	Z	

I = 9, E = 5, A = 1, O = 6

9 + 5 + 1 + 6 = 21

21 = 3

NUMBER ONE

- This born leader is confident and purposeful.

- A high energy level, determination, and ambition create success.

- This person does not give enough time or energy to the love life.

NUMBER TWO

- This person is sensitive, kind, and vulnerable, and needs emotional security.

- This individual has an overwhelming desire to give to and care for others.

- The Number Two person is a gifted healer or therapist.

NUMBER THREE

- This eternal optimist has a good sense of humor.

- A tough exterior hides a fear of rejection or abandonment.

- This individual makes a great parent, reliable partner, and wonderful friend.

NUMBER FOUR

- The Number Four person is shy and sensitive, so shuns the limelight, preferring family life.

- This born homemaker needs comfortable, spotless surroundings.

- This individual may build or improve a home.

NUMBER FIVE

- Relationships can bring problems, but friendships succeed.

- The Number Five person dislikes authority and restriction.

- He may study alone or find others to share their views.

NUMBER SIX

- Love is the key to happiness, but it may take time to arrive.

- The Number Six person puts the needs of others first.

- This individual needs praise and support to feel totally confident and relaxed.

NUMBER SEVEN

- The Number Seven person is happy to be alone.

- This individual could be a mystic and philosopher.

- Close relationships make this person uncomfortable.

NUMBER EIGHT

- The Number Eight person feels secure when in control.

- This good organizer becomes moody when things don't go his way.

- He is often unable to relax and let go.

NUMBER NINE

- This good organizer loves variety, challenge, and changes of scene.

- A problem solver, the Number Nine person is a good mechanic who likes to know how things work.

- He can have a clinical attitude toward relationships.

NUMBER ELEVEN

- The Number Eleven person makes a decision and sticks to it stubbornly.

- Despite being self-reliant, this person needs to feel wanted.

- Ideals and principles are important to this individual.

NUMBER TWENTY—TWO

- If this person gets a grip on reality, he can achieve whatever he wants.

- He is a charming companion and great friend.

- The Number Twenty-two person can create an atmosphere of peace and harmony.

LIFE NUMBER

For this section, you need to use the date of birth. You can reduce this to two digits, as long as the numbers fall between 1 and 21. If we look at the following two examples, you will see how to do this.

Date of birth: January 2, 1970
Addition: $1 + 2 + 1 + 9 + 7 + 0 = 20$
The number 20 is below 21, so it is within the range.

Date of birth: May 2, 1982
Addition: $5 + 2 + 1 + 9 + 8 + 2 = 27$
The number 27 is outside the range, so we reduce it by adding 2 and 7 to make 9.

NUMBER ONE

- A purposeful leader.

- A creative person, if there is sufficient opportunity.

- One who likes to exercise authority.

NUMBER TWO

- A well-balanced and cheerful individual.

- One who is sensitive to the needs of others.

- An individual interested in partnerships, teamwork, and politics.

NUMBER THREE

- A versatile and adaptable person who is easily bored by routine.

- One who needs freedom to travel and explore.

- An individual with intuition and common sense, which lead to success.

NUMBER FOUR

- A hardworking, sensible, logical, and methodical person.

- An individual who can be materialistic and fussy.

- Either a very traditional person or a real reformer.

NUMBER FIVE

- A lively, creative, and artistic individual.

- An excellent communicator who may teach or write.

- A lover of travel who balances this with home and family life.

NUMBER SIX

- An individual to whom harmony in the home and among friends is vital.

- A very hard worker who sacrifices himself for others.

- A person who can succeed in entertainment, writing, the arts, or the health industry.

NUMBER SEVEN

- A spiritual, sensitive, intuitive person.

- One who is into alternative therapies, psychism, and mysticism.

- A caring individual who is also attracted to film, poetry, and story writing.

NUMBER EIGHT

- An ambitious, self-sufficient, persistent individual.

- A powerful leader or tycoon.

- One who is interested in justice and honesty.

NUMBER NINE

- A creative, spiritual, compassionate individual.

- One who is interested in the theater and the arts.

- A person who can be religious, possibly too much so.

NUMBER TEN

- A self-motivated individual.

- A person who is not easily influenced.

- The head of a family and king of his realm at work.

NUMBER ELEVEN

- A determined personality who can get things done.

- One who has high principles, but for whom selfishness may spoil good intentions.

- A successful risk taker, as long as he is not too self-indulgent.

NUMBER TWELVE

- An emotional person who has a tendency to sacrifice.

- One who is associated with the unseen and secrecy.

- An individual for whom it is essential to grasp educational opportunities.

NUMBER THIRTEEN

- An individual whose number is linked to positive power when used wisely.

- One whose life can entail change and rebirth, upheaval and trauma.

- A person for whom it is essential to be adaptable.

NUMBER FOURTEEN

- An individual whose life is characterized by challenge and movement.

- One who is fortunate in financial matters.

- A subject who must be cautious when taking risks.

NUMBER FIFTEEN

- One who is associated with magic and power.

- An individual whose life holds luck and good fortune.

- A subject whose life will be dramatic.

NUMBER SIXTEEN

- One for whom events may not go according to plan.

- A passionate, volatile person.

- An explorer or inventor or just an impulsive and rash individual.

NUMBER SEVENTEEN

- A lucky number for games that can also bring fame.

- This number brings power and success through achievement.

- A subject who may have a difficult life.

NUMBER EIGHTEEN

- One whose life is linked with the home and family.

- A person whose life path is sometimes difficult.

- An individual who must balance material and spiritual matters.

NUMBER NINETEEN

- A successful, good-humored, and happy individual.

- Someone who is good for speculation and recognition.

- A person who will have many dealings with children.

NUMBER TWENTY

- One whose life is ruled by fate and karma rule.

- An individual whose life will never be boring or dull.

- A person who will succeed with plans and new projects.

NUMBER TWENTY-ONE

- This number denotes power, success, and achievement.

- One whose life is marked by success and karmic benefits.

- A subject who will succeed if he is persistent.

7

DESTINY NUMBER

The destiny number shows your destiny and life purpose based on your personality and potential. Find this number by adding together the letters in your full name as it appears on your birth certificate, including any middle names. Keep on reducing the numbers until you end up with a number between 1 and 9, or 11 or 22, then look up the interpretations.

Here is a repeat of the system and the example that appeared in the introductory chapter.

1	2	3	4	5	6	7	8	9
A	B	C	D	E	F	G	H	I
J	K	L	M	N	O	P	Q	R
S	T	U	V	W	X	Y	Z	

James Robert Pearson

James: 1 + 1 + 4 + 5 + 1	= 12
Robert: 9 + 6 + 2 + 5 + 9 + 2	= 33
Pearson: 7 + 5 + 1 + 9 + 1 + 6 + 5	= 34
	79

Now we reduce this number by adding 7 and 9 to make 16.

Then we reduce the number again by adding 1 and 6 to make 7.

Thus, James Robert Pearson's destiny number is 7.

NUMBER ONE

People with this number like to be in charge of events, and they can be bossy and dictatorial. This is the number of leaders who hate it when people tell them what to do or when others try to restrain or restrict them, because they like having their own way. They need to be the center of attention at all times. These individuals are highly creative, and they love to be at the head of a large family. They can be demanding in relationships, and their passionate, sexy nature frequently leads them to look for affairs outside marriage or partnership.

NUMBER TWO

These people are well balanced, diplomatic, and level-headed, and they create an atmosphere of calm in situations that others find hard to control. They are tactful negotiators, they are protective of others, and they keep their own counsel, so they do well in any job that requires these special talents.

They are loving and protective toward their families, although some of their loved ones find them patronizing and overconsiderate, which makes them feel stifled by the over-whelming attention. A relationship with the right partner can be passionate and successful. These people prefer to be in a partnership in their personal lives and in business.

NUMBER THREE

These people are determined to succeed in everything they decide to do, and they are bright, cheerful, and enthusiastic. When unhappy or disappointed, they hide their feelings behind quick wit and humor, so they make excellent actors—and they love an audience. In a similar way, these individuals also make great salespeople.

These people often feel lonely, and they may not get things right in the area of personal relationships; part of this is because they need freedom while also needing desperately to feel loved and cherished. They are flirtatious and attractive, but despite their talent for attracting interest, this doesn't satisfy them, because what they really need is someone who will be happy to share their life in a loving relationship. Their best attribute is their sense of humor.

NUMBER FOUR

These organized people spend their lives making lists. They are methodical, efficient, and systematic, and they make wonderful employees. Many of them remain single throughout their lives, frequently preferring the company of animals to close human relationships. However, they enjoy being involved in local or community matters.

If they marry, it will be to improve their financial or social position. While they can be relied upon to be faithful, they can be difficult to live with, because they cannot compromise, and they feel that they have to control every situation and everyone around them.

NUMBER FIVE

These subjects are hard workers and excellent communicators who need change and variety to function well. They can become restless if required to concentrate on something they don't want to do, and if this happens, they will find a way of escaping from their restrictions. Travel is vital to them and they move around a great deal.

Where relationships are concerned, they love the thrill of the chase, and they are flirtatious. In some cases, they take their time about finding a partner or they find it hard to settle down with one partner. They have a strong sex drive, so when the novelty wears off with one partner, they may move on quickly to the next romantic challenge.

NUMBER SIX

These people can be very successful in a business or any enterprise of their own because they push themselves, work hard, and have very high standards. They can be perfectionists who channel a great deal of energy into doing things properly and also into making money.

They love to make others happy and content, but their attitude to relationships is not always traditional. They are attractive and loving, but sometimes they are so busy working at their job or keeping up impossible domestic standards that they don't notice when their partner needs love and affection. Loving and faithful, they demand that their partner always look good. This is partly because these people are into fashion and clothes themselves, to the point that they may be interested in following a career in the fashion world. They are happy to give their partners money for clothes, cosmetics, and beauty, and if money is tight, they will learn to design and make clothes for themselves and their loved ones.

NUMBER SEVEN

These dreamy, philosophical folk want to save the planet, adopt a cause, or embrace mysticism. They excel when they work in a group, and especially in a teaching or helping role. Music and the arts are important to them, and listening to music might ease their tensions or allow them to sing along and express their romantic feelings.

Although very loving, they cannot stand a clingy partner, as they must be free to follow their particular star. These individuals are renowned for their mood swings, and this makes them hard to live with. These attractive, physical, sexy people find it hard to relax into a relationship, so they often leave their partners wondering what they really feel about them or what they really want.

NUMBER EIGHT

This is the number of the hardworking business tycoon who thrives on responsibility and makes a success of himself. He expects much of himself, and he has absolutely no time or tolerance for the failings of others.

These individuals are highly organized at work, but they don't leave enough time to focus on their relationships, which may suffer and then wither away. Weaker people are drawn to their apparent strength and energy, but then feel short-changed when this subject suddenly becomes cold and uninterested in them. Frankly, these individuals are often too ambitious to put enough effort into long-term partnerships or marriage, so sooner or later, their partner will drift away and look for love and affection elsewhere. If they can find a partner who shares their passion for work or who is happy to work in the same business as them, they can be passionate, happy, and contented—and make their partner happy as well. They do make an effort to give time to their children, and most are good to their parents as well, as long as the parents are not demanding or clingy.

NUMBER NINE

These highly organized people have such a finely tuned level of intuition that they can make excellent split-second decisions that appear rash to others. They are impatient and they want everything now! They will not wait for anyone or anything. They enjoy variety and challenges in life and in their work.

In partnerships, they are exceptionally loyal and can be a tower of strength in any crisis, but it can be hard for them to form one-on-one relationships, as they feel more comfortable as part of a group. They make warm, caring, and generous friends and lovers.

NUMBER ELEVEN

Communication is important to these people, so they often find employment in the media and in films. They are excellent writers and teachers who have a naturally creative streak. They make good leaders, and they are unlikely to let their employees down, because they have high ideals that they rarely compromise.

They have much to learn about living with others, because they love power and being in control. If they concentrate on a partnership, they will be successful, but it is hard for them to avoid putting their careers first. They have the knack of making influential friends, and this helps them in many different spheres of life.

NUMBER TWENTY—TWO

Personal magnetism makes these individuals stand out in a crowd and attract attention, and they often use this to get ahead in their career or job. Idealistic as well as practical, these people are usually successful and they do especially well in design work that combines special sensitivity with an artistic eye. Obvious outlets for their talents are architecture and engineering, or perhaps designing computer software or games.

They are remarkably successful in relationships, and they have many admirers. They prefer to be faithful to one partner, although this feeling may not always be reciprocated.

8

KARMIC NUMBER

To find the karmic number, add the name number and life number. In this case, it is best to use the name on your birth certificate added to your date of birth.

This shows where your faults lie and where you can work on yourself to enhance your soul's progress. Naturally, you can choose not to improve your behavior, but the chances are that you will suffer some kind of karmic payback as a result. This also gives you an opportunity to assess the karmic value of other people—as long as you can discover their full birth name and birth date, that is.

NUMBER ONE

These subjects must watch the tendency to control everything and to dominate others. Childhood and adolescent problems may be resolved as life progresses, and ambitions can be realized, leading to material security and even wealth. They should try to balance the material and spiritual sides of everything. However, they rarely acknowledge their true spirituality and nor do they understand those who do.

NUMBER TWO

Emotional outbursts can create problems, and moodiness can overcome logic. These people may become martyrs, so they should try to be less passive. They can make mountains out of molehills and become upset over trivial matters. However, they are good partners who are supportive of their families, but they must learn to make time to relax and enjoy themselves and their loved ones. They must guard against blindly trusting others, as they can attract people who are not always as honest and trust-worthy as they should be.

NUMBER THREE

These individuals must guard against being conceited and boastful, and they must strive to be realistic. Business ventures often succeed because their enthusiasm and extravagance makes them successful risk takers. They can be very good company, but they can sometimes spoil this by their stubborn natures and a tendency to be envious of others and greedy where possessions and money are concerned. They are quite capable of spending their partner's money on themselves if they get the opportunity. On the plus side, they are good to their children.

NUMBER FOUR

The main life lesson for these individuals is endurance through a life of uncertainty and change. They are cautious, which is no bad thing. However, they can have fixed opinions and ideas about what other people should or should not do: this can cause unnecessary problems with colleagues or relatives. They must learn self-control and consistency, and they must try to be less complacent about their own failings.

NUMBER FIVE

The life lesson for this number is perseverance and attention to detail. These honest, sincere, adaptable and witty

people lead lives full of movement and travel, either because they choose jobs that involve travel or because they are restless. Some move house or even move from one country to another due to circumstances that are beyond their control.

NUMBER SIX

These people must guard against sarcasm and taking a cynical attitude. They can be condescending to others, self-righteous, and possessive, but in spite of this, they tend to be popular and to have many friends. They make many sacrifices for their loved ones, and others can rely on them because they have an ingrained sense of duty.

NUMBER SEVEN

These subjects must learn to use the many opportunities that come their way and to not give up when things go wrong. They should use their compassion and vision for the benefit of others as well as themselves, and avoid drifting into escapism. They should embrace alternative ideas and mysticism, but without becoming fanatical about these things.

NUMBER EIGHT

The need to learn patience is most important here, and these people should guard against becoming overmaterialistic. They should make an effort to create a social life and time out for fun and frivolity. They must avoid being too demanding of others or even too hard on themselves. They can hurt themselves by harboring resentments.

NUMBER NINE

These individuals often prefer their own company or the company of animals to living in a partnership. That is fine, but there are times when they must cooperate with others at work, even if they work alone. They may also need to create harmony in a family situation—even if they only have to do this at Christmas or other family occasions. Their colleagues, relatives, and friends know that they can turn to them in a crisis.

NUMBER ELEVEN

Other people may see these people as intimidating and superior when in reality they are highly creative and blessed with enormous stamina. They rarely fail in anything they undertake, but their high principles may tip them over into obsession.

NUMBER TWENTY-TWO

This is a number of perfection. People with this number will happily work for nothing for a cause they believe in, but they should learn to maintain a balance in life in order to give their idealism a realistic basis. The most positive attributes they possess are the gifts of enlightened wisdom and humanitarianism.

HOW TO USE NUMEROLOGY
FOR SIMPLE PREDICTION

You can discover what any year will hold by adding your month and day of birth to the year in question. For example, if you were born on February 15, 1985, but you want to see what life will be like in 2007, drop the year of birth and add the month and day to the year in question. Then reduce the final number to a single digit. Here is an example:

Birth date: February 15, 1985

Year date: February 15 plus 2007

Addition: 2 + 1 + 5 + 2 + 0 + 0 + 7 = 17

Reduction: 1 + 7 = 8

This person will be in a Number Eight year in 2007.

YEAR NUMBER ONE

This is the start of a new cycle, so ensure that your affairs are in order. You may spend more time alone than you have for some time past, so you must now examine your own needs and concentrate on making an effort to improve your circumstances. You may find yourself living in a new area, changing jobs, or making new friends now, so you must try to put the past behind you and concentrate on the future. The many changes that come your way this year may not be easy to live with, but they will turn out for the best in the end and you will learn many new things along the way. The extra energy and drive that you have now will help you to cope with your various new situations.

Settle any outstanding matters that remain as soon as you can, and you will find that during March, any uncertainty will have disappeared. Between April and November, you will be busy with new projects. Listen to what others have to say and avoid behaving in a stubborn or arrogant manner. Any new people who enter your life this year will be part of your life for some time to come, so choose partners and friends wisely.

YEAR NUMBER TWO

It is not a good idea to make major decisions this year, but you should keep the resolutions that you made last year. Things may not seem to be moving fast enough for your liking, so try to develop patience and to establish basic harmony in your life. You will need to take other people into account and to work with them rather than against them. This means developing a certain tact and diplomacy. Other people may have their own ideas and they may not wish to change them.

This should be a year of good health, and you can expect some opportunities for travel. There may be some difficulties to face in your love life, but you should work hard to improve this if it is at all possible. Indeed, you must work hard to establish partnerships of many kinds this year.

If you fancy a change of address, it would be wiser to wait until next year. It is possible that you will decide to take up a new creative activity this year, and if this is the case, it may assume importance in years to come. Whatever your long-term aims are, keep them on track, but try to take some time off and to relax whenever the chance presents itself.

YEAR NUMBER THREE

You may reap the rewards of past efforts, and you could even expect a windfall or two this year; even a gamble might pay off. Do not allow setbacks or negative and envious people to spoil things for you. You will be busy, and you might even find yourself in the public eye at some point. A burst of creativity could bring new opportunities. Take them—you should be full of enthusiasm and feeling optimistic. You can have a very productive and happy year if you are determined to make the best of everything.

If you are single, you can expect social gatherings, happiness, fun, and romance to come your way. This year, all partnerships and friendships are well starred. You may decide it is time for a new image, so keep a careful eye on your diet and brush up your appearance and your wardrobe.

YEAR NUMBER FOUR

Material needs are important this year, so get down to business and work hard. Set yourself targets or goals and ensure that you do all you can to reach them. This is not the year in which to put too much energy or time into your social life. Lay the foundations for the future by making plans, clearing away anything that wastes your time and energy, and preparing to start afresh.

You will find yourself thinking about money, as you may well have a number of unexpected expenses. Be careful to save whenever you have the opportunity, because financial stability will be important, but do not become greedy or obsessed by money concerns.

Your home will be the focus of much of your attention, and you may make long-needed improvements there. Alternatively, you may arrange or rearrange your mortgage or some other loan for home improvements or extensions. The increase in your career status and earning power might be behind this, as you will now be in a position to improve your living quarters. The summer months will show progress in all your affairs, though, so you will need to be patient, and you will need to keep an eye on health matters.

YEAR NUMBER FIVE

This is a year of movement in your affairs. If there is something in your life that is not working, this is the time to change it, so you may move house, change your job, or travel, but you must think any decisions through carefully. Luck will come your way during the middle part of the year, so go ahead at that time and don't allow others to hold you back.

This is the number of communication, so you will have a full date book, and many meetings, telephone calls, e-mails, and invitations. The opposite sex will find you attractive and interesting, so all the activity will make you feel as if you are in a whirlwind. Go everywhere, meet everyone, and experience everything this year. People will take notice of you. You may start some new venture or get promoted at work.

Expect the unexpected throughout the year, and remember to take every new opportunity and chance for advancement.

YEAR NUMBER SIX

The main emphasis this year is on your personal affairs, so you must attend to any domestic and emotional issues that are outstanding. You may experience matrimonial problems or difficulties with friends, or perhaps there are outstanding legal matters to be resolved. Any friendships that have been under a cloud will improve during this year.

If you have been struggling to make a dicey friendship or a love relationship work, you will realize that you can do nothing more to improve it. This means that you may lose a friend or give up on a bad relationship for good. Whether this is the case or not, if you are alone, you could meet someone new, because you will want to be content and settled. The greatest issues are related to balance and harmony, and this is a very important year for love.

YEAR NUMBER SEVEN

Step back this year and have a period of relaxation and rest. This will give you a chance to take stock of your life and consider yourself more than you normally do. Concentrate your energy on your own welfare, and, for once, take care of your own health and requirements before those of others. A short spell away on your own or periods of meditation may be what you need this year.

Travel is highlighted this year, so you will find yourself taking short trips. If your work involves travel or if it concerns the travel industry, you can expect to have an especially good year. Unexpected opportunities to travel may take you by surprise and will allow you the opportunities you need to learn new things.

Do not spend too much time worrying about the material aspects of your life this year, because this is a time for philosophical or spiritual issues. Do not be surprised to discover a new interest in mysticism, magic, and spirituality. If you are already working in this field, this will be an extremely rewarding year. Even if such matters are of no interest to you, you may find yourself spending more of your time and energy helping others throughout the year.

YEAR NUMBER EIGHT

Rewards for past efforts will become apparent during this year, and although they may be slow to arrive, they will eventually come along. You can expect financial and business successes. Advancement of all kinds and promotion at work are highlighted throughout the year.

If in the past you have been unwise or reckless, things will catch up with you and you may experience losses and a new feeling of instability. You might receive a welcome windfall, but it is equally possible that you will lose your job or have financial problems. You will win and lose in the game of life this year.

Elderly relatives may become more part of your life, and older people in general can find that they have important roles to fulfill. Property matters will be important—many people may be involved in buying or selling property, possibly in connection with older relatives.

Romantic issues come to the fore, as this is an important emotional year. Some would call this a karmic year.

YEAR NUMBER NINE

For many people, this last year in the cycle will be a time of reflection, so you will look at your situation and assess those things that you really need to change. You will also start to look at ways of improving your position or making personal strides in both practical terms and spiritual ones. Having said this, you may not be able to implement these changes or improvements until next year, because this is a time for consolidation or preparation rather than for change.

Do not be surprised to discover yourself acting impulsively and feeling that you must make some decisions quickly this year. However, take care to consider all your options so that you do not regret later what you have done, because it is likely that your judgment is not at its best. This is not the time to make drastic changes to your personal life, and it is important to try to retain a sense of balance.

Make plans for the future, reflect on what you have achieved, and spend time thinking carefully. Things that are no longer relevant will start to slide away this year. You could feel depressed and insecure at times, but without this knowledge and understanding, you cannot begin the year that follows this one with a clean slate.

Think less of the past and more about the future. If you can view the year in terms of progress in the future rather than endings and loss in the present, you will discover that many of the events that are happening will turn out to be for the best. The solid friendships you have built over past years will be important to you this year, and you should show your partner and friends just how much you value them. Do not become oversensitive or obsessive or lose your sense of perspective.

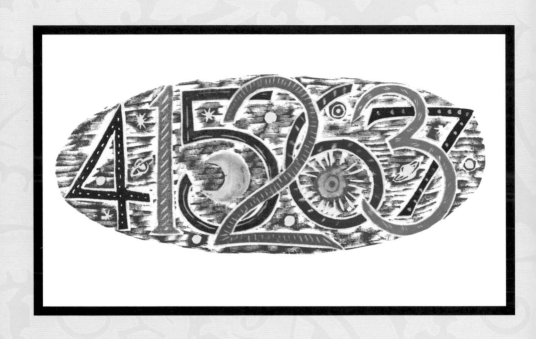

10

SHORT-TERM FORECASTS

Here are some quick and easy ways to work out your personal vibe for any month, week, day, or even hour. Reduce your birth date to a single number and add it to anything else that you want to examine in order to find the combination.

MONTHS

Add your life number to the number of the month and the reduce the sum to a single number. Thus, if your life number is 6 and the month is September (the ninth month), add 6 and 9, which equals 15. Then 1 and 5, which equals 6.

DAYS

Add your life number to the day of the month. Thus, if your life number is 1 and the day you want to look at is the eighteenth, add 1 and 1 and 8.

HOURS

Use a twenty-four-hour clock and add your life number to the time. Therefore, if your life number is 4 and you want to see what will happen at 7 o'clock in the evening (which is the nineteenth hour in the twenty-four-hour system), add 4 and 1 and 9.

Now you can look up your prediction number in the following pages to see what is likely to happen.

PREDICTION NUMBER ONE

A Number One energy brings opportunities for a fresh start. If you need to tackle something difficult, you will have the energy and optimism with which to do it. This is a good time to sign a contract, finalize an agreement, or start a project. This is also a good day for chatting with interesting and intelligent people and getting some input and ideas from them. You will not be short of positive ideas, but you must analyze them to see whether they will hold water. Avoid haste and impctuosity if you can, and try not to walk all over other people.

PREDICTION NUMBER TWO

This is a good time for continuing a project and consolidating what you have done so far. This is also an excellent time to mingle and cooperate with others, to listen to what they have to say, or to seek help from them if you need it. Partnership issues should go well, but sometimes a Number Two time can bring conflict or issues that you should talk over with others in a reasonable manner. Try to find time to relax a little during the course of this period if you can.

PREDICTION NUMBER THREE

This is an excellent time for creative thinking and for coming up with problem-solving ideas. If you are into artistic matters, these will go well. You should avoid behaving in an

obstinate or irritable manner with others, and if you need to stand up to unpleasant people, you should try to do this in a direct and assertive manner and not simply by digging in your heels. This should be a great time for parties or socializing. If you can do something other than work, do so now. If you need a meeting or a discussion or if you need to take a short trip or to go shopping, this is a good time for such activities.

PREDICTION NUMBER FOUR

This is an excellent time in which to get jobs done in a practical and constructive manner. If you need to make a special effort or to attend to specific details, do it now. This is not such a great time to start a new project, but you will be able to break the back of one that has been hanging around for a while. You should also reach out to all those with whom you have to deal or cooperate, and to pay attention to personal relationships and partnerships. The only problem is that you might ride a little roughshod over others in your haste to accomplish everything.

PREDICTION NUMBER FIVE

Number Five times are particularly changeable, so you may choose to change direction now and try something new. It is no good making plans, because you will need to go with the flow at this time. Short journeys or even longer trips could well be on the cards during this spell. You could meet interesting people or find yourself having new and different experiences. Phone calls, e-mails, or letters could take you by surprise, but in general, all matters regarding communication will go well. Try teaching someone how to do something, or learn something new yourself at this time.

PREDICTION NUMBER SIX

Despite the fact that this number is often associated with quite hard work, there is evidence that you will be able to take some time off in order to do some of the nicer kinds of shopping. By this, I mean shopping for something other than food or other basic items. Listen to the music you like and do the things that make you happy. This is a good time for love and affairs of the heart. Nevertheless, work will take precedence during some part of this period, as will doing things for your loved ones.

PREDICTION NUMBER SEVEN

Matters concerning love, passion, affairs of the heart, and relationships come to the fore now. Concentrate on your love relationships today if you can, even if it means neglecting some of your chores, because there will be something in your personal life that needs attention. This is also an excellent time in which to go on an inward journey and to do some thinking or to contemplate spiritual matters. If you have any studying or research to do, this is the time for it. Try to use some part of this rather quiet period for a little relaxation.

PREDICTION NUMBER EIGHT

Financial and business matters rule when this number is in operation, so if you need to sort out your finances, pay bills, and reconcile your checkbook, get down to this now. Business matters will flourish, and if you need help or advice from those in positions of authority, this is the time to ask for it. In addition, you may be able to resolve a financial problem. Your intuition will be spot-on, so you can sit back, observe others for a while, and try to fathom their underlying motives and agendas. At this time, you might prefer to spend some time alone. One source of ancient wisdom says that if you are likely to hear of a death, it will be on a Number Eight day.

PREDICTION NUMBER NINE

This is a good time to end a cycle of events and bring jobs or certain aspects of your recent life to completion. You may want to look back on what you have achieved and make plans for the future, but you cannot start anything new just yet. It would be best to avoid taking action or making specific decisions in a Number Nine period if possible. Finish any outstanding jobs and get ready for the action to start again later. If there is nothing much going on in your life or at work, use this time to clear out cupboards, sort through your paperwork, and throw away out-of-date stuff that is cluttering up your space. A specific piece of advice for this period is to be honest and fair in all your dealings with others.

11

ABOUT NUMBERS

I thought it would be a nice idea to tell you a little about the history of numbers and how they have come to be used in numerology.

LANGUAGE AND NUMBERS

The earliest form of numbers came from the country we now call Iraq, and especially the fertile area around the Tigris and Euphrates rivers. This is where the first towns and cities came into existence—other than those in ancient China, Burma, and Peru. Up to that time, humans lived a simple hunting or farming existence and had no need to keep records. Cities brought the first forms of business, which in turn brought about the need to account for animals that people bought and sold, or the need to account for the purchase and sale of grain and other goods that were stored in a central location. The earliest writing in this area was called cuneiform, and it was basically an enhanced bookkeeping system.

Egyptian and Chinese writing derived from pictograms (pictures) that eventually became connected to sounds or words. As time went by, the sounds' names and uses of these words changed their meaning, gradually lost their pictorial form, and drifted into looking like early forms of writing.

LETTERS AS NUMBERS— HEBREW AND ANCIENT GREEK

An early type of writing that depended upon actual letters was Hebrew. Hebrew has also gone through various incarnations over the millennia, but it has not changed as much as many other forms of language. Aleph is still aleph and bet is still bet—although even within modern memory, there are people who have pronounced bet as beth or even base.

The Hebrews didn't have a separate number system, so they simply used the letters of the alphabet as numbers.

The Kabala is a late invention among Jews. Some of its roots may go back almost two thousand years, but in essence it comes from the Middle Ages or even later. Each sephira of the Tree of Life is numbered. For those who want to take the Kabala further, as Madonna has, the "pathways" between the sephirot are also numbered (sephira is singular, sephirot is plural).

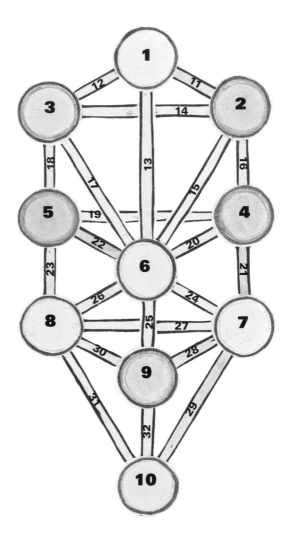

The Kabalistic Tree of Life

The ancient Greeks used a system and alphabet similar to those of the Hebrews; here are a few letters for comparison.

Hebrew:		Greek:	
Aleph	א	Alpha	α
Bet	ב	Beta	β
Dalet	ד	Delta	δ
Lamed	ל	Lambda	λ

THE ROMANS

The Romans also used letters as numbers, and we call these Roman numerals. You can see these at the top of the Tarot cards in some decks. Here are a few Roman numerals.

M C L X V I I I

M = 1,000

C = 100

L = 50

X = 10

V = 5

I = 1

IX = 10 minus 1, therefore 9

XI = 10 plus 1, therefore 11

IV = 5 minus 1, therefore 4

VI = 5 plus 1, therefore 6

As you can see, both of these systems were cumbersome, and neither included a zero. This made mathematics difficult, as zero is a real number—not just a vacuum.

TRUE NUMBERS

The number system that we use in the West today is called the Arabic system, or Arabic numbers. This system actually came from India, but Persian and Arab traders used it because it was simple, it worked for math, and it was universal. It wasn't attached to any particular nation, such as the Roman, Greek, or Hebrew nations, so it had no national or religious connotations.

Amazingly, the Arabic system is based on a circle, which means that the whole number system is set inside a zero.

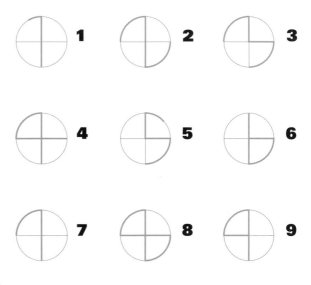

The Arabic number system

SHORTHAND

Shorthand writers know that the basis of the Pitman short-hand system is also set in a circle with certain letters fitting into it, but the concept is more complex than the Arabic number version.

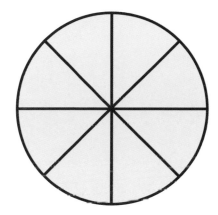

A circle with a cross inside it and diagonal lines

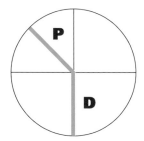 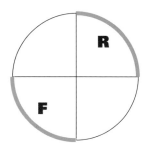

The letters P, D, F, and R in Pitman shorthand

12

RELATIONSHIPS

This chapter is mainly about love relationships. These may include an enduring marriage, a long-term friendship, a passionate fling, or a passing fancy. Some combinations are good for a work or business connection, so I have included a few of these as well. This is mainly aimed at women who want to give their partners (or potential partners) a critical once-over—but the guys will also want to take a sneak peek.

The number of stars next to each number shows the most successful partnerships, but even those with few stars can work. Sometimes opposites attract, and relationships that don't appear at first glance to have any potential can work out. Only those with no stars at all have no real chance of anything more than a short-term fling.

For this calculation, work out the number of the name that you usually go by. For example, if you are a 2 and your partner is a 7, find number 2 and look for number 7 in the number 2 section. Then do the same for the person you love. Find your relationship number in the following pages, and your partner's within each section.

NUMBER ONE

3 * * * *

You share enthusiasm and a determination to succeed. While you will compete with each other, you will also enjoy lots of passionate lovemaking. You will also have many good laughs together.

4 * * * *

This combination works, as both of you are practical, logical, and keen on keeping up appearances, but you want a family and your partner may run a mile from the idea of being part of a family unit.

7 * * * *

You both share an interest in setting clear limits, and you share an appreciation in the outdoors, nature, and the romance of wild places, so you would both enjoy energetic outdoorsy pastimes.

22 * * * *

Although a Number Twenty-two is a dreamer and you are a doer, the potential for a long-term bond is excellent as long as you give each other the space that you both need.

1 * * *

This relationship promises lots of fun, as you are both cre-ative and passionate, but you would both want to take charge of every situation, so there might be one too many clashes here for a long-term romance.

8 * * *

You will appreciate this hardworking partner who takes responsibility and who can handle success, but you both like to be in charge, so it may not work out in the long run.

5 * *

On one hand, your hardworking partner will be happy to spend hours chatting with you, but this partner needs the thrill of the chase, so this might only work as a short-term attraction.

6 * *

Number Sixes love to make their partner happy, but they prefer staying at home to going out and making their mark in the world, and this isn't your idea of fun.

9 *

Both of you are impatient, but you are both loyal and strong in a crisis. There is little chance of a successful love connection, but a working arrangement might succeed, as there is a measure of mutual respect.

2

This relationship would emphasize too many differences, so it is best avoided.

11

An attraction is unlikely, and this relationship wouldn't work on a career basis either.

NUMBER TWO

5 * * * *

You both love to chat, debate, talk about what you read or see on the television, and gossip, so you would never have time to become bored with each other.

8 * * * *

You respect this person's serious attitude to work and to making a success of things. You will help your partner to achieve success, and you will then both enjoy spending your partner's money.

2 * * *

Lots of fun and passion are the keys to combining for these naturally attractive people. There may be an element of competition in this relationship.

9 * * *

This combination makes loving partners, and both can be a tower of strength in a crisis. You will be passionate lovers, as long as the association includes work or business as well as romance.

11 * * *

This link works well, as long as you both give plenty of time to it. Each of you has high ideals that you hate to compromise. Your shared interests and passion for life—and for each—other will make this one a success.

22 * *

You both have many admirers and are usually successful in all kinds of relationships. This could be great fun, with lots of passionate moments.

6 * *

You are both loving and faithful, but there is a great deal of emphasis on both of you looking good, so there may be clashes about who spends what on their appearance.

7 * *

You will appreciate your partner's loving nature, but you may not be able to cope with the mood swings. Attraction will not be enough to sustain a long-term bond.

1 *

These people always want to be in charge, and there are just too many differences to create a good relationship.

3 *

Although your partner would do his best to make this succeed, his tendency to be flirtatious would upset you.

4

You want family life, but this partner isn't interested, so no chance here.

NUMBER THREE

6 * * * *

This would make a stunning affair, but you have a traditional attitude to marriage, while your partner does not. This pairing makes for an excellent business combination, though, as you would set the pace and your partner would deliver the goods.

9 * * * *

You are both loyal and you both enjoy variety and change, so there are good possibilities for a successful long-term link.

1 * * * *

This person wants to be the head of a family and the center of attention. This can be a fun romance with lots of passion, but you would eventually become fed up at having to play the part of an admiring audience.

3 * * * *

You share the same sense of humor and need for affection, so this can be a passionate and successful choice. You would give each other the space that you need.

5 * * *

Although loving the thrill of the chase, this partner will work hard to make a relationship succeed. You share an interest in reading, thinking, talking, and traveling, so you would certainly have a fun time together.

7 * *

Although this partner is renowned for moodiness, he wants to love and be loved, but his weird attitude will leave you wondering. There is an attraction, but is it enough?

8 * *

Home life seems to come in second place unless this relationship combines romance with work or business. There could be a clash of personalities.

2 *

You may feel stifled by a partner who fusses, hovers over you, and restricts your freedom. Too many differences suggest little chance of a successful partnership.

4 *

If this partner wants to marry you, it is because you fit into a particular pattern that he has in mind. Is he after you for your house or your money? Maybe not, but maybe he does have his eye on only his own interests.

11 *

You need attention and you need to feel as if you are in charge, and this person won't give you enough attention or allow you to make decisions.

22

You will want to get out of this one almost before you get into it, but a Number Twenty-two will cling, so it is best not to get involved in the first place.

NUMBER FOUR

1 * * * *

You can manage this sexy, passionate person, and the opposites in your natures will always keep each of you interested, so this has excellent long-term possibilities.

4 * * * *

Two Number Fours could hit it off well together, since neither enters into a long-term relationship lightly. Your mutual love of method, system, and efficiency might drive other people mad, but you understand each other perfectly.

7 * * * *

Renowned for their mood swings, these attractive, physical, sexy people may puzzle you, but as long as you give each other loads of space, this can work well.

2 * * * *

This will work as long as your partner doesn't try to crowd you or control you, but the passion that you share will make this a fun event—even if only a short-term one.

6 * * *

Loving, faithful, and successful, these people put their energy into making money, which suits you to a tee. You could have lots of fun together amassing a fortune. This would also work on a business basis.

11 * * *

Given time to concentrate on the bond between you, and bearing in mind that your partner might be a control freak, this could work out well. Healthy competition would create a fun-filled, passionate romance.

22 * * *

Although your partner will have his head turned by too many other admirers, the passion between you could keep the spark alive. This pairing would create a useful working partnership.

8 * *

This entrepreneurial type is well-organized but frequently intolerant and cold in a close relationship. The clash of personalities will soon send you off to find true love and affection elsewhere.

9 * *

Although loyal and faithful, good in a crisis and capable of making split-second decisions, this partner wants everything now! Attractive, maybe, but this looks more likely as a working arrangement.

3 *

You might appreciate this person's sense of humor, but little else, and you have little in common. This works best when it is nothing more than a casual friendship.

6

What on earth would you find to talk about?

NUMBER FIVE

2 * * * *

This can be a successful and passionate long-term link as long as your partner doesn't patronize you or hem you in. He means well and he is loving and loyal.

8 * * * *

Your partner is a responsible, successful individual who can make you very happy and contented, especially if you share an interest in business. This pairing holds excellent possibilities for an enduring situation.

11 * * * *

You are both excellent communicators who are willing to put the effort into learning how to make a long-term bond successful. Provided career matters do not take first place, this is a good bet for both partners.

3 * * *

Although they love an audience, these subjects will do their best to make a partner happy in the security of a long-term permanent connection. If they feel loved and cherished, they bring a sense of fun and passion to this link.

5 * * *

A strong sex drive makes for a passionate relationship with lots of laughs. Both of you are romantic and addicted to travel, so this is well worth putting some effort into.

7 * * *

In spite of the initial attraction, take care not to allow your partner to draw you into competitive power struggles and spoil the chances of long-term success. If you share the same interests, that will help you along.

1 * *

Your partner is demanding, bossy, creative, sexy, and passionate. If you don't mind the fact that he may be having flings outside the relationship, and if you are willing to play second fiddle, that's fine. Otherwise, avoid this clash of personalities if you are looking for a long-term situation.

9 * *

This partner is loyal and passionate, but he can be impatient and rash, while thinking that he is actually sensible and well organized. Do you want such a challenge? There could be a bad personality clash here.

4 *

Faithful and predictable in love, this may just be another control freak in the making. Attractive, perhaps, but remember that these people often marry for money or remain single all their lives.

6 *

This partner can be a perfectionist taskmaster who fails to notice when a partner needs love and affection. There is very little chance here for a successful long-term romance.

22 *

Although this may be the ideal faithful partner at first glance, this person's personal magnetism attracts too much attention from others. Do you want to spend the rest of your life, being sidelined by a crowd of admirers, with someone who wants freedom but who also refuses to let you go?

NUMBER SIX

3 * * * *

You stick to a partner, and this person needs that, so you can give each other the reassurance that you both need. Your partner's fantastic sense of humor and desire to make you happy will make for an enduring love relationship.

5 * * * *

If you and your partner are at a stage in life when you are both prepared to settle down with one person, this will work. You will have loads to talk about and many shared hobbies and interests. Otherwise, this would make a great loving friendship. It would work well on a business basis too.

4 * * * *

This loyal partner is a tower of strength in a crisis. He loves challenge and variety, and this also works for you, but you may feel harassed at times because this individual hates to be kept waiting.

6 * * *

Two Number Six people together will understand each other instinctively. They will work hard to create a loving and faithful partnership with lots of passion and just a hint of competitiveness. However, both can become very down-hearted on occasion, so each of you would have to prop the other up at times.

8 * * *

Combine this personal association with work or a business and it will be successful. Both partners will be happy and content with equal responsibility for the love and passion that makes a romance sizzle.

1 * *

Number One people love being the head of a large family. If that's not what you want in a partner, you should avoid this person, who always needs to be in the limelight and at the center of attention.

2 * *

You may feel stifled by the attentiveness of a Number Two person, who is always loving and concerned for the family and those who rely on him. It is likely that a clash of personalities could emerge, which would make you both unhappy in the end.

11 * *

Because they love to be in control, these people have a lot to learn about one-on-one situations. Although you may be mutually attracted, you would probably resent your partner's need to put a career before all else.

7 *

This person's real goal is to save the planet, and he is happier with a group of like-minded friends than in a close relationship. Although warm and caring, this person makes a better friend than marriage partner.

9 *

This can make a great working arrangement, as your partner would think up the ideas for you to carry out, but it would make an exhausting love partnership.

22

This clever and creative person has great potential for success as long as he is alongside someone who can pick up the pieces when some of his ideas fail. As a romantic attachment, you would soon bring each other down.

NUMBER SEVEN

1 * * * *

You are so different that you could fit together very well in a way, as each of you will complement the other. Your partner is a natural leader while you are an idealistic dreamer, but both of you are creative, sexy, and passionate.

4 * * * *

Although this individual, who loves to be involved in the community and is passionate about animals, often prefers to remain single, there are good possibilities for a successful relationship. This is someone who will be faithful and predictable.

7 * * * *

These two people will instinctively understand each other, which is a good start in any partnership. Fun and passion, along with many shared interests, make this a good link.

22 * * * *

This person has exceptional talents and abilities, and you would appreciate this. In spite of having many admirers, this individual will remain faithful to one partner. You are unlikely to resist this person's charm. This pairing has an excellent possibility for a long-term bond.

5 * * *

Although they hate to be restricted, in a partnership with a Number Seven, this is unlikely to be an issue. You both love to travel and enjoy romance, and you share a strong sex drive. A fun relationship with lots of laughs and long-term potential is likely.

9 * * *

This might be fun on a short-term basis, but you like to go with the flow while your partner wants to do everything yesterday, so you would soon get on each other's nerves. However, your mutual love of variety and challenge brings spice into this relationship, so despite the odds, this has a good chance of lasting.

2 * *

This could work in its own strange way—say, if you both took up an interest in alternative therapies and psychic matters; otherwise you might find your partner a little too conventional for your tastes. However, you will appreciate your partner's passion.

3 * *

Your partner would demand more attention than you want to give, so in spite of a mutual attraction at first, this is unlikely to work out. In addition, this partner is surprisingly flirtatious, and this may not work in a permanent situation.

11 * *

You both have high ideals, and neither of you can compromise, so you both have a lot to learn about how to make a relationship work. Power gives this partner a kick, because he needs to be in control. This is unlikely to be a workable partnership.

6 *

You prefer to go with the flow, while this partner needs to focus on details and get everything done right—and right now. Although these people love to make others happy, this would not be a comfortable relationship for either of you, in spite of a superficial attraction.

8 *

Only a relationship that includes work or business has any chance of success.

NUMBER EIGHT

2 * * * *

You are ambitious and you focus on your career, while this partner is oriented toward looking after the home and family. This could be a wonderful combination, as you would each have a defined role—you as the breadwinner and your partner as the homemaker. More important, you can keep your thoughts and feelings to yourself whenever your partner gets into a state and loses his temper.

5 * * * *

This lover's amazing sex drive, love of travel, and preference for short-term projects make them great fun. An excellent communicator, he will work hard at a keeping love alive, so this is a good bet for a demanding person like you. There is every possibility of a highly successful long-term relationship here.

11 * * * *

Good at making friends, career-minded, and interested in the media world, these people often work in film or TV. They have the highest ideals and are willing to learn how to manage love and marriage, as they can focus on a partner's needs. This is an ideal mate for you.

1 * * *

Even if they sometimes behave like tyrants, these people are irresistible, especially to ambitious Number Eight, who needs a strong partner to manage his family life. This highly creative, sexy, passionate lover could be an ideal choice.

6 * * *

The genuine ability to make a partner happy makes these attractive individuals loyal long-term partners. They are perhaps not always traditionalists where marriage is concerned, but you may appreciate that, especially as there would be plenty of fun and passion, and a hint of competition.

8 * * *

This makes a wonderful business arrangement as long as you each have your own sphere of activity and don't compete with each other. As partners, you must each have your own career interests, but when you are not at work, you will have an instinctive understanding, many laughs, and many passionate moments.

3 * *

Bright, cheerful, and enthusiastic, this partner is determined to succeed. He may be both pushy and flirtatious at the start of a relationship. Although you both start out with the best of intentions, there may be a clash of personalities, which bodes ill for the long term.

4 * *

If you are both into farming, horses, running a kennel, and that kind of thing, you could certainly work well together, but there is not enough to sustain a loving bond between you.

22 * *

In spite of an initial magnetism between you, these individuals are more concerned with getting ahead in a career. A short-term business venture will work because you have the financial acumen and your colleague has the practical knowledge that you can use. As a romance, this would not last more than five minutes.

7 *

You are on two different planets. This person is emotional, dreamy, and happy to live and work in a somewhat chaotic environment, and all that would drive you nuts. There is little chance of a long-term relationship being successful.

9

These people would rather be one of a group than make sacrifices for their partners.

NUMBER NINE

3 * * * *

You both love doing things spontaneously, and you both think on your feet and move very quickly. You appreciate each other's efficiency at home and in business. Your partner will make every effort to make you happy, and while he's a little flirtatious, in the security of a loving bond, this may not be an issue.

6 * * * *

Your partner is only really happy and secure when in a loving relationship, and his perfectionist tendencies would not upset or bother you. Indeed, you could concentrate on your career in the knowledge that your partner is taking good care of the family, the home, and your possessions.

2 * * *

Well-balanced and levelheaded, these protective, tactful individuals can create an atmosphere of calm and contentment, but this link could also be amusing and full of zest, with just a hint of competition.

7 * * *

You will find this loving person ideal as long as you give him space for his many outside interests. Your partner may be moody sometimes, but he is attractive and sexy, so this could be a passionate affair that can stand the test of time.

9 * * *

You may both appear to be rash and impatient to outsiders, but you understand each other perfectly in a long-term committed partnership. Both are loyal, and both have the kind of backbone that enables you to cope with any crisis. You might both enjoy working together in a capacity where you need to cope with anything that can happen.

11 * * *

Communication is the key to success in loving relationships, and you each have something important to contribute. You may seek to compete with each other at times, but this should not prove an insurmountable problem for either partner.

4 * *

Although they make wonderful employees, be aware that these people are loners. They often prefer not to make committed relationships—except with their pets. There may be passion and fun at first, but this is probably not going to turn into a satisfying long-term partnership.

5 * *

It is important to understand that these people can easily become restless, so if you want your partner to stay behind while you follow your pursuits outside, you will come home one day and find your dinner in the oven, but nobody home!

22 * *

If you like to have someone to share an occasional vacation with or to help you out when you have a sticky problem to discuss at work, you will become friends. Otherwise, there is little to keep either of you interested.

1 *

The moment that this powerful and self-centered personality starts laying the law down to you is the moment that you leave, so there is little chance of success.

8

This partner will snap at you and expect you to take it. You may put up with this behavior once, but when it happens again, you will vanish into the mist.

NUMBER ELEVEN

5 * * * *

You share an interest in travel, people, education, and keeping your mind active. You will respect your partner's skill in do-it-yourself activities and his devotion to his career. Add a sexual attraction to this and you have a good chance of making this work.

8 * * * *

These ambitious people are not easy to live with, but you have what it takes to make this bond work. For one thing, you are both creative and capable in your different ways, so you will always have some project or other to talk about. This would also make an excellent working relationship.

2 * * *

This loving and caring personality is also levelheaded, balanced, and diplomatic. If you share hobbies and interests and have lots to talk about, this makes a great association that has a strong element of friendship as well as love.

9 * * *

Although these people like to be part of a group, they understand the importance of personal love and commitment and they will make extremely generous long-term partners.

11 * * *

You both have an oddball side to you, and as long as your interests are similar, you will get along very nicely. Although competitive, this person is lively and passionate, loving and appreciative of family life, so it would work well.

22 * * *

This person has probably had a difficult childhood, so he will appreciate being in a close and loving relationship. He is generous and kindhearted, so his occasional outbursts of temper or silliness won't upset you.

4 * *

A combination of these numbers will make a successful business partnership, if you deal with the creative or manufacturing side of things and your partner handles the bookkeeping and finances. In a personal relationship, the lack of passion or real interest in each other makes it a non-starter.

6 * *

Here is a hard taskmaster who expects his partner to channel a lot of energy into making money. Although they love to make others happy, there is every chance that they will put their career first and may not notice when a partner needs some love and affection. There could be a better partner for you.

7 * *

Although these people make loving partners, and they are sexy, attractive, and physical, their frequent mood swings may leave you wondering just how important the relationship really is. Not an ideal choice.

1 *

This would make a dynamic business partnership, although even here, you would both fight for supremacy. You are both so focused on your career aims that a personal relationship is almost impossible to imagine.

3 *

Because they often feel lonely even in a close, loving relationship, these subjects can be flirtatious and needy. This is not a good partner for you, as the link would fall apart the moment you tried to regain your power in the situation by controlling your partner.

NUMBER TWENTY-TWO

1 * * * *

Always in charge, sexy, and passionate in close relationships, this partner can be an excellent choice. This individual is never tempted to stray from a long-term commitment or to indulge in affairs outside a marriage. It is not a problem for you that this charismatic, creative individual demands to be center stage and sometimes behaves like a tyrant. This has the makings of a first-class long-term relationship.

7 * * * *

Although it might seem that dreams of saving the planet or adopting a cause, or embracing mysticism and philosophy, are most important for this partner, he is loving and kind, and it may work surprisingly well on all levels. This is a good choice that should bring happiness.

2 * * *

You are both interested in having a partner and in family life, so there is much potential here. If you fill the house with lame ducks and children, your partner may grumble, but he will be happy enough as long as he has a workshop of his own so that he can design things and fiddle around to his heart's content.

6 * * *

This person will go a long way to make you happy and content. Loving and faithful, the most Number Sixes demand is that their partner looks good and doesn't turn the house into a mess. There could be much worse to live up to.

11 * * *

Good communicators and excellent teachers and writers, Number Elevens make influential friends easily and will put effort into making a relationship work. They will appreciate the clever way that you make the house and garden look good.

4 * *

You need far more reassurance than this person can give you. He would make a fine friend and a good workmate, but nothing more, really.

8 * *

You need love, attention, affection, and reassurance, but this person is too busy building an empire somewhere to have the time or patience to devote to your needs. He just cannot sit down and listen to you while you talk about your feelings. This is not an ideal partnership.

9 * *

This person is something of a loner, so he will not understand your need for a close relationship and he will not prop you up when your self-confidence takes a nosedive. You may appreciate his company during a holiday romance, but not when it comes down to living together.

3 *

These people are too needy to be able to maintain a successful relationship with a Number Twenty two. Don't even bother trying; it will end in tears all around.

5 *

This person looks sexy and attractive at first glance, but he may not be ready to give up having a good time and settle down with one partner and maintain a marriage or committed relationship.

22

Although there will be some basic understanding here and possibly even initial attraction, there is a personality clash that is likely to be horrific. So, unless you like to have a really good argument every single day, find someone else.

13

THE NUMBER GRID

The number grid adds a little something extra to your reading, and for this you should use the number that you get from your date of birth—that is, your life number. Each row of numbers has a particular energy when you read the columns vertically and horizontally.

	PHYSICAL	INTELLECTUAL	SPIRITUAL
CREATIVITY	3	6	9
EMOTION	2	5	8
MATERIAL	1	4	7

THE KEY TO THE GRID

The first vertical row (1, 2, 3) relates to the physical body.

The middle vertical row (4, 5, 6) relates to the intellect.

The last vertical row (7, 8, 9) relates to the spiritual nature.

The bottom horizontal row (1, 4, 7) relates to the material world.

The middle horizontal row (2, 5, 8) relates to the emotions.

The top horizontal row (3, 6, 9) relates to creativity.

The diagonal line (1, 5, 9) relates to communication.

The diagonal line (3, 5, 7) relates to effectiveness.

INDIVIDUAL NUMBERS

Each number has a meaning of its own. You have already seen these ideas expressed in the first chapter on single numbers, but now you can see how they work both singly and as part of the grid.

1 Personal creativity
2 Feelings
3 Resources
4 Instincts and logic
5 Expansion and senses
6 Intuition and theory
7 Setting limits
8 Transformation
9 Spiritual creativity

INTERPRETING THE GRID

Check out the vertical, horizontal, and/or diagonal lines that contain your number.

Vertical line 1, 2, 3

These numbers describe the physical world, so these individuals know their identity; they can feel with the conscious mind and can perform actions.

Vertical line 4, 5, 6

The numbers describe the world of the intellect, abstract thinking, creative thought, imagination, and theory.

Vertical Line 7, 8, 9

These numbers describe the world of the spirit. They relate to the unconscious mind and spiritually creative talents with which the subject has been endowed.

Horizontal Line 1, 4, 7

These numbers are associated with the material world, so they focus on thinking things through logically and getting them done in a practical and realistic way.

Horizontal Line 2, 5, 8

These numbers focus on emotions, the unconscious mind, the feelings, and intuition.

Horizontal Line 3, 6, 9

These numbers concern creativity, so a touch of genius—or at least great creative talent—might be indicated. These numbers also refer to karmic rewards from previous lives.

Diagonal Line 1, 5, 9

These numbers emphasize the value of communications, a willingness to learn, expansion and use of talents, spiritual creativity, and the ability to create new life.

Diagonal Line 3, 5, 7

These numbers denote the ability to act sensibly and a desire to learn and to understand how to set limits.

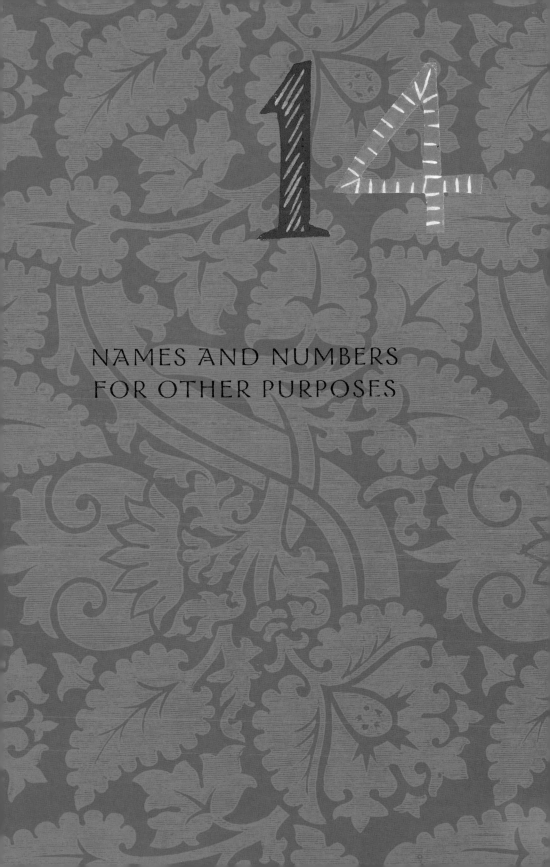

14

NAMES AND NUMBERS
FOR OTHER PURPOSES

A friend of mine married for a second time, and her husband told her that every automobile he had ever owned had a license plate number that added up to a three, six, or nine. This didn't include the letters on the plate, just the numbers. He hadn't deliberately chosen cars with these numbers; it had just happened. Since being together, they have owned various secondhand vehicles, and at one time, they even inherited one from a relative who died. Sure enough, every single car that her husband drove had a license plate number that added up to three, six, or nine— even the inherited one!

This phenomenon is not as uncommon as one would think. There are people who seem to be followed around by a certain number, which they come to think of as their lucky number. There doesn't seem to be any rhyme or reason for this, as these numbers are not prominent in their numerology, astrology, or any other system—they just appear to exist for some weird reason of their own.

HOUSES AND ADDRESSES

Let us now get back to numerology. It is interesting to see how your house number might affect your life, and the same goes for a business address. This is a brief rundown of the energies of each number from one to nine. Naturally, if your number is longer than a single digit (and, of course, most are) you must add the numbers together and then reduce them to a single digit in the usual way.

NUMBER	HOUSE NUMBER INTERPRETATION
One	A fresh start, a new lifestyle, independence and self-starting; also, getting a concept or business off the ground
Two	Partnerships, relationships, cooperating with others in private life and in business
Three	Creativity, childbirth, and passion, but also arguments; good for business enterprises
Four	Consolidation, family life, earning and saving money, putting down roots in a marriage or a business
Five	Movement, travel, visits, visitors, and plenty of conversation; in business, marketing and communication take precedence
Six	A new relationship, making a new home for someone you love, work, and a need to be on top of everything; in business, sometimes too much to do
Seven	Great for a vacation home or place to relax, to meditate, or to develop psychically; not good for business—too vague and nebulous
Eight	Money will pile up here, but only after a period of hard work; even if you are not a businessperson, you will become businesslike and systematic here
Nine	You will stay here long enough to bring a relationship or child rearing to an end; this number encourages you to keep going until it is time for a new phase to begin—then you will move again

VEHICLES

Now let us take an amusing look at your automobile, van, truck, or motorcycle license plate number. First, see which single digit it adds up to.

NUMBER	VEHICLE INTERPRETATION
One	This vehicle's number is fast and reckless, so watch out for speeding tickets
Two	Two likes company, so you will rarely be alone when driving this automobile
Three	You will think up creative ideas while driving this vehicle, but difficulty in diagnosing faults will be an ongoing problem
Four	This is a stately, respectable, but boring vehicle that will last forever—your mother will be happy that you are in a safe car
Five	This sporty number longs to move, so you will spend more time driving than you have in the past
Six	Shopping, chores, carting children about, and giving lifts to neighbors and relatives characterize this workhorse
Seven	Keep your mind on the road and listen to lively music, because this vehicle could put you in a trance
Eight	This is a really hot number, so your automobile is either a prestige sporty vehicle—or it just thinks it is
Nine	You will put up with this dreadful old banger while working your butt off to save for something better

INDEX